JOSEPHINE BAKER
SWIMMING POOL

Tim Suermondt

MADHAT PRESS
ASHEVILLE, NORTH CAROLINA

MadHat Press
MadHat Incorporated
PO Box 8364, Asheville, NC 28814

The Library of Congress has assigned
this edition a Control Number of
2018965355

ISBN 978-1-941196-82-3 (paperback)

Author photo by Jasmine Yuen

Cover art by Marc Vincenz
Cover design by Marc Vincenz
Book design by MadHat Press

www.MadHat-Press.com

First Printing

for Pui and the Devil Sisters

Table of Contents

A Cautious Optimism   1

Josephine Baker Swimming Pool   2

The Pull of *Telenovelas*   3

A Revolution, After All   4

Just Life   5

"John Wayne" in Vietnam   6

Les Gobelins   7

At Eighty-Five My Father Wins His Last Bet
   at the Track   8

Like Evangeline Oak   10

Autumn and Patience   11

One or the Other or Many   12

Remembering the Ones Who Didn't Come Back   13

Red Roses Auvillar   14

The Yellow Shirt   15

Cultivating the Women   17

By the City   18

Change It to Solace   19

I Like Sparrows but I'm Putting My Foot Down   20

Staying the Courses   21

Snow and Snow   22

Sometimes What's Right with the World   23

All the Amplitude We Need   24

The Circumference of The World   25

The Chair I Carry Around   26

When the Bull Stops Fighting   27

"surprise, nuance, immediacy, wit, a flash of steel"   28

The Blue Horse   29

A Last Act of Wisdom   30

Paris Often Gets in a Little   31

Oran   32

When the World Really Ends No One
    Will Announce It   33

The Sail of the World   34

A Letter from a War Zone   35

The Yellow Car at Auvers   36

At Cemetery Montparnasse   37

Believing in It   38

The Next Leg   39

In an Alleyway of History   40

Standing That Counts   41

Small Streets   42

Hopeful in Utrecht Tonight   43

I've Changed Some People Say   44

I Stand Almost at the Edge of the Ocean
    but I Pay It No Attention   45

Saving the World   46

Out of The Dark   47

Jimmie Collins   48

To the Poets Who Won't Get a Drop of Ink
    When They Die   49

The Quiet of Paris   50

The Tram Turns onto the Last Street	51
It's Only the Universe	52
Inspector Watanabe	53
They're Off	54
The Old Idea of War, 2237	55
It Does Matter	56
Do Some Fishing along the Seine	57
Revolution Street	58
September	59
Piaf	60
Marconi Beach	61
Bob Dylan Wins the Nobel Prize	62
Proust	63
Shouldn't Be Much to Ask	64
"Letter to a Young Poet"	65
Spending Part of New Year's Eve Watching a *Three Stooges* Marathon	66
Waiting for My Wife Who's Gone to Do a Quick Errand	67
The Cavalcade of Children	68
After the Election	69
The First Day of Summer	70
Whistle	71
The World Isn't Ending	72
Acknowledgments	73
About the Author	75

What would life be like if we didn't
dare measure ourselves against it?

—Vincent van Gogh

A Cautious Optimism

A fearless optimism would be better,
but we do have to take what we can.

The fault lines between the large *H*
and the small *h* of history are eroding

every minute, falling chips often
feeling like a spray of shrapnel.

Yet today the sky was clear, the night
placid with a few stars, the air smelling

a little aromatic and couples on benches
silhouetted in the branches and leaves of trees,

gratitude humming Beethoven who insisted
"if you know my music, you know happiness."

Josephine Baker Swimming Pool

My wife and the others plunge in,
    sluice the water like the most elegant of porpoises.
Even my landlubber heart feels the charm,
    the elemental power of water, wishing
I had the ability to join the swimmers,
    if only to scissor back and forth once.
Through the ceiling dome, a Paris rain,
    a band of crows circle in the dart-blue sky,
Josephine Baker's spirit among them—I believe
    in such things, despite the world's admonishment
and every evidence to the contrary.
    My wife is out of the pool, toweling herself off,
slowly swaying her hips, her own Banana Dance
    cool among the marble and the immortality.

The Pull of *Telenovelas*

How can we not be moved
when the blonde *dueña* says

"Oh Roberto, you and I
cannot be dull and sad."

And though most of the characters
look more like models

than, say, hard working *rancheros*—
we like them still

and want to follow their adventures.

The couple escapes from danger,
the couple kisses by the fountain—

and the cameras pan to Mexico City,
its lights ablaze, and because

there is so much tragedy so many
people are dancing in the streets

to life and justice, and the sky
crisscrossed by the shadows of birds.

3

A Revolution, After All

We talked politics so long and so hard
that we finally quit to concentrate
on the constitution of the sky, noticing
the buds on the trees growing, the sun
confidently starting to show itself.
We decided to cook slowly until days end
and toasted our wine glasses to the red
cardinals and Cuban doves who'd flown by our
windows, turning and soaring with the grace
and guile of jet pilots every revolution adores.
We put the political books back on the shelf
and went to bed and dreamed of tomorrow
which we believed would be a few degrees
better and allow us to sleep in late and in peace.

Just Life

I see the moon moving slowly
by my study's window—shepherd
moons on the job, those tugboats
to the ocean liners of the universe.
I hear cello music, then muted rap
turning to silence. A couple walk
their dogs on the edge of the park
and everything I lost is coming back—
with flourish and no trace of sadness.
I push aside papers and finish a book,
back, back in love with the impossible.

Tim Suermondt

"John Wayne" in Vietnam

What many of the middle school children called me
while giving an enthusiastic peace sign—all of them
amazed to see an American this far out, many miles
away from the territory of the tourists.
The girls in long white dresses, boys in white shirts,
ties and black shorts—I pointed in the Mekong's direction
and said "Many years ago over there …" and all of us
started laughing when a cow mooed and the sky turned an even
brighter blue, blue as the always a little doleful but beautiful river.

Les Gobelins

In this Paris neighborhood
I read a book on The Resistance

to strengthen my poor French.
As I close the book the sun starts to set

and two pigeons land on the window-
sill, shaking some rain off their wings,

watching me closely like philosophers.
Buoyed by the valor of the past, I'm ready

to go out and order take out from a number
of establishments, ready to carry my baguette

of language with firmness and pride
down the boulevard, even singing a French

song I never realized I knew, doing a nifty
spin move past a man wearing a LeBron James

jersey who says something in French,
cheering me on, cheering me on, I'm certain.

Tim Suermondt

At Eighty-Five My Father Wins His Last Bet at the Track

He places his money
on a brown beauty,

    Swirling in Dough—

I opt for *Kentucky Bourbon*

a former Pimlico champion
who comes up dry,

still running the course
as every other horse finishes.

When we cash his ticket
my father counts each bill

with deliberation as though
they might disintegrate—

"I'm getting old," he says,

    "I'm getting old."

He stuffs the money deep
into a pocket of his lucky

beige pants—"I'll buy us
a hot dog…Which way do we

go, son? Which way do we go?"

Tim Suermondt

Like Evangeline Oak

Should I ever have the desire to paint on canvas
I'll start off simple—painting not a country
but a room, a chair, a window. Young women
by a window worked wonders for Vermeer—
the light and shadow, the ubiquitous pitcher
and the mouse, unseen, loafing along the wall.
"What a wonderful room," I'd like people to say,
a room that can withstand joy and heartbreak,
a room you don't have to be a genius to live in.

Autumn and Patience

I feel a little foolish letting my wife
corral me into picking peaches

in this public orchard miles from
civilization, a robust pizzeria.

Yet I soldier on and even my wife
says "You've been so patient"

and for a moment I suspect there
may be hope after all, maybe including

world peace in the mix, tragedy sitting
under the trees, promising no harm

will befall anyone on this day.
"We can go soon if you like," my wife

says, demonstrating she can employ
magnanimity when she so desires.

"It's okay," I say just as a white light
leaps and bathes me as if I were somebody.

Tim Suermondt

One or the Other or Many

At times I'm sure the universe is expanding,
at times I'm sure it's contracting.

This is akin to my believing in God
when things are going well,

not believing when they're not—
the elasticity of certainty as frustrating

as it is magical with possibilities.
That boat on the river—is it going somewhere,

everywhere, nowhere? Who knows?
Do I see women in bikinis on the deck

or a couple of old salts hunched along the railing?
This slow dancing with my wife

in the kitchen—is it for me, for her, for us both?
One step too far, one step not far enough

can change the earth as much as any amount
of ergs dropping like eggs into a bowl—

precisely random, care and abandon,
spinning the plates like the stars.

Remembering the Ones Who Didn't Come Back

Usually when it rains—
though never of monsoon proportions.

A young woman tramps down
a dirt road with an old ox

whose bell around its neck
can be heard even with a transport

plane roaring overhead. A soldier

holds his rifle with one hand,
and waves to the woman with the other.

She waves back: a touching scene
the world is still capable of.

We keep our umbrellas close by now—
they trained us so well.

Red Roses Auvillar

The roses *are* big and beautiful but, ultimately,

sad as the faded glory of Marshal Pétain, inconsolable

because they cannot be with us as much as they would like,

as much as we would like, clustered above the old houses,

churches, pizza parlors, lost like us, like Horst Bucholtz

and Leslie Caron, like Chevalier on his rainbow sweeping

the clouds away but only in a dream, Zidane head-butting

his opponent for the love of his mother, Camus and Moulin

romantic despite the cruelty on earth, never-ending despite

the angels of a better nature Lincoln could not deliver, red

roses dying in winter after the affairs of summer, red roses

like a woman you can always be with but never have, a woman

equal to the world you will lose as well, gratitude in the night

searching for you on the smallest street, searching everywhere.

The Yellow Shirt

I know—way too loud,

but I'm wearing it today
because the world is not acting

the way I want—a lunkhead

protest, probably, yet one
that couldn't be more sincere.

And there I am walking it through

the good and bad part of town,
the entire length of public parks,

along the river glutted with freighters

and getting five nibbles of admiration
to offset the looks of perplexity.

And there I am in the early evening,

stepping into my apartment, taking off
the yellow shirt and putting it back

in the closet, I sense, for good.

The yellow shirt won't see the stars
bunched tight tonight, but I will—

a huge advantage I'd do well to cherish.

Cultivating the Women

Or are they cultivating me, while
they take over the apartment?

Some dress so fine the word *dazzle*
will not do. Some dress more mundanely

and one at the end of the couch wears
only underwear, crossing her legs, proud

to be provocative yet a little aloof.
So many women huddled in the tight space

but we wouldn't change it for the world—
this planet as strange to itself as it is to us.

Is trying a tango step by the kitchen island
the foolish endeavor I hope it is?

And is that a Roman legionnaire we see
flying smoothly by, red as the night sun?

Tim Suermondt

By the City

for Rachel

The sun shines like a blister
On the knee of a long ago childhood.

Pelicans and cranes fly over the harbor—
Adults on the pier toss hard-crusted breadcrumbs skyward.

A day so beautiful it's sad.
A day so sad it's beautiful.

What do we know of anything? Though we try.

The final loveliness of the night—
I see you coming.

Change It to Solace

Mourning will visit—inevitably,
dark as a night in a Polish village.

The wind can whisper
some of Hyam Plutzik's lines

and other balms will wrap themselves
around the lemon trees

along the road, the red houses in town—
a lantern in a backyard always on.

Tim Suermondt

I Like Sparrows but I'm Putting My Foot Down

A one-year prohibition on sparrows in poems
makes sense and says justice,

especially those who always flyover
endless fields of yellow brilliance

and pick out the rooftops of charming cities
to nest and ride out the winter.

They do smack a bit of paradise, a perfect
excuse to bow our heads in awe,

but lately a bow is not on my agenda
and the dying are making too much noise

for wonder to carry the cloudy days.
I wish the dodoes were still with us, I wish

poets would put them in their poems,
I wish for so many things that will never be.

A cadre of sparrows just flew by—the bastards!

Staying the Courses

The sway of the world
always enthralls me, even
when the world disappoints.

I love the mixture of gravitas

and sexiness—the mind in a book,
the hands holding a pair
of thin, light-colored panties—

what a night for astrophysics

and human beings. I walk the wide
boulevards, the side streets reeking
of red, exotic roses—my feet moving

to a rhythm I actually believe is mine.

Tim Suermondt

Snow and Snow

It keeps showing up like a complaint
no one has an answer for.

And as it does the flimsy tarps
surrounding the apartment under

construction flap like specters who see
no way out, pitiful in their hopelessness.

A few dogs leap in the whiteness,
their owners looking grim as soldiers

at Stalingrad while I hunker in the study,
a hermit lately every day, every night.

Sometimes What's Right with the World

Just enough breeze to cool things down—
pale blue sky courting a lonely but comely cloud.
Trains moving slower than old beetles—
cars and trucks on the elevated highway, crisscrossing
like ants with racer's legs.
Even the twenty-story building standing at attention
wants to be humble—the tenants know magnificence
when they see it.

Tim Suermondt

All the Amplitude We Need

Easy to say the world is fractured—
when so much of the world is,
but as my wife and I walk through,
around, under and over the city
we wallow in its hubbub, going out
of our way to follow what might prove
to be extraordinary, a glitterati of sights
even at the end of an avenue, the beginning
of a side street fogged by a spewing manhole,
perfume and other odors tying themselves
around us like lariats while a swan escapes
the park, moving between cars and buses,
momentarily jolted as we are by the junkie
yelling from a second story window, asking
for money no one will give him, his gaunt
face breaking into light from the sunray
he lets comb what hair he has, his nervous hands
moving in bizarre but beautiful pantomimes
before he goes inside, beaten yet again, fractured,
which is where my wife and I came in, vowing
to be blushed by gratitude and never giving in.

The Circumference of the World

A hummingbird, a thimble,
a runway bigger than many towns.
Slacks hung in the closet, panties
draped over the sink, a museum
of antique cars, a bowl of chocolates.
The milk tree, the endless dilapidated
cul-de-sacs, the mornings announced
by the bored rooster, nights by
the crickets brash as opera singers.

Tim Suermondt

The Chair I Carry Around

Built of sleek black wood
and a velvet seat cover—

the best of the new world
and the old. I carry it, now and then,

for the grandest of reasons: I want to.
And much to my surprise people

have come to accept this, little fuss
being made as I walk the streets.

A woman said "That's a lovely chair"
and asked if she could buy it—

no, no, no I'd never sell. I still hear
those who say "I can't do this" I can't

do that" and here I am carrying a chair
I cradle like a gorgeous baby or

a lovely violin. If I can do it so can
they. That chair forlorn by the doorway—

pick it up and give it a try. We'll wait
for you in the park, by the gilded fountain.

When the Bull Stops Fighting

So does the matador.
He drapes the cape over the bull
and says "Let's get our wounds
cleaned up, old friend."
Together they limp out of the arena—
the crowd unable to decide to boo
or cheer does neither.
Side by side they travel, the matador
and the bull, down an old, long
street El Greco could paint with his
eyes bandaged over twice.
The two shimmer in the heat of the day
and disappear, the cape on the ground,
the cape a saint shall bless, then destroy—
what is heaven but what we leave behind?

"surprise, nuance, immediacy, wit, a flash of steel"

Surprise is the easiest:
how I seem to remember everything about the city
and how it seems to remember everything about me,
despite our long years of separation.

I open the windows in my found apartment
and sunlight makes a beeline to the tiny area
I've chosen as my study—I follow its glow to the chair,
sit and lean back, already preparing myself

for the good, hard work, the dreams and the imagination
to come, feeling the sweet steel of one word: *home*—like
honey on my tongue—feeling my heart adjusting itself
to its new furniture being arranged so, so beautifully.

The Blue Horse

It wasn't really blue, but at seven years old
it was the color I assigned. My father,
who had the sincere idea that buying a horse
out in the dusty green farmland of Encino
might be good for me and my mother, decided
he might have been mistaken—the blue horse
left to the next available bidder and dreamer.
I thought at the time that the horse looked
downcast, a bit sad at not going home with us.
Rather ridiculous I know, but even now
whenever I feel left behind by the government,
the death of friends or abandoned by women
I believed I would love forever—I remember
the blue horse, my father holding me slightly
aloft to help me rub my fingers along
its ultra-smooth mane, recalling how brave
it tried to appear as we slowly drove out of sight.
A damn shame—it was truly a beautiful animal.

Tim Suermondt

A Last Act of Wisdom

My father packed a small suitcase,
said "I'm going" and vanished in the air,

leaving behind his coat—its pockets
filled with candies—on the bed.

He always knew how to be
quietly spectacular. He always knew

how to do what he thought was right.

Paris Often Gets in a Little

Enough times for me to say
I surrender to the city's charms
like the most starry-eyed tourist.
But let the Tower Eiffel and all
the other beauties speak for themselves
while I walk through a long afternoon,
along a line of rarely used train tracks
and make my way into the vastly ignored
park of Saint Cloud with its grotesque
statues and fountains blackened beyond
repair by thick layers of soot and grime,
a nightmare of Versailles soothed in the crisp
breaking light of this fall day I need like mercy.
A tall teenage boy actually streams Piaf
from his blue and orange boom box, the only
sparrow who's put in an appearance, the three
of us alone and together now, indefectible.

Tim Suermondt

Oran

from a terrace a woman's
voice cries ooh!
—Italo Calvino

Even in the distance,
while I try to rub the palm leaves
and the long night out of my eyes,
I can see she's beautiful,
delicately poised in her white robe.
Her ooh! sounds sweet as the sea air,
the sea that takes a few more grains
from the foundation of the Grand Hotel
and sends them all over the world.
I stagger a little through the square
but keep what little dignity I have intact,
heading in her direction, both my hands
for effect and thanksgiving on my heart.

When the World Really Ends No One Will Announce It

So relax. Let the emissaries of everything
bring what they want.

There will be the worst—war insists.
Yet the best will not be shy—love insists.

Prim and proper is fine, but keep allowing
the oddball to find its serene equations:

   Look at the sun trying to put on pants

   Look at the moon tying on a scarf

   Look at the angel riding a skateboard

exactly like she dreamed,
her wings smudged, bent just as she prefers.

Tim Suermondt

The Sail of the World

Is always passing by—

a bit lonely but full of life—

heavy as the universe,
light as silk,

almost being immaculate.

Just now it's come over

a long-legged crane
perched on the bridge railing

and over a small brigade

of construction workers

ramping up the high rise
with sweat and expertise.

A Letter from a War Zone

The letter is imaginary but the woman who wrote it is not:
      I saw her
on television, standing beside a burnt-out building,
      waving as if
she had seen a friend or a lover coming her way
      after months
of separation. In her letter she documents the travail
      and tragedy
but also mentions how sometimes after a shelling
      the light
will waft through the streets "like a thin blanket of magical
      honey"
and the moment a red cardinal appeared, claiming its part
      of the rubble.
My friend saw a red cardinal land and preen
      on the windowsill
of his hospital room, minutes before he was wheeled
      into surgery.
I'm waiting for a red cardinal too, confident it will come
      in my direction.
The letter ends "One day you'll bring me chocolates
      and I'll greet you
with roses"—I fold the letter and wedge it between the pages
      of a great
book, another author who tried to sneak in a handful of grace
      amidst the divisions
of sadness, doing his best with the only weapon he ever had.

Tim Suermondt

The Yellow Car at Auvers

Still hugging the narrow space between the road
and the brown apartment building—
exactly as it did when I first saw it seven years earlier.
This is planned coincidence à la Sebald, this is the clearing
from the forest towpath, from the wheat fields,
from the gravestones of Vincent and Theo
and those known only to loved ones and legions of crows.
This is the assurance of continuity in the midst of change
rolling us like boulders down a hill—this is my wife now,
a yellow-stemmed rose between her teeth, motioning me forward.

At Cemetery Montparnasse

Wake up,
the earth loves you.

Look at the shoes it brought
so you can walk forever.

Tim Suermondt

Believing in It

My wife and I take an afternoon walk
along the river, mixing in small talk
with a little big talk.

We love looking at the tall, but not too tall
buildings of the city that seem
to have been made for this skyline.

We embrace and kiss like the teenagers
standing in front of a cluster of white
sailboats do, and all the bad actors

are washed away, everywhere.
It's so simple: a walk, a river, a city,
a wife and husband—the world making up,

teasing us again into believing in it.

The Next Leg

To my surprise the greatness of mankind
triumphed with no irony attached.
What the next leg will be I have no clue
but I see a little girl dressed as an angel,
her winged arms stretched out
for the entire play and a boy, in a navy
blue suit, banging a drum, relishing
the noise. Perhaps everything does come
around again, the sun, moon and earth,
those slivers of silver and gold, of mercy.

Tim Suermondt

In an Alleyway of History

A man sharpens a pencil
or a knife blade.

A woman is bereft
or stifling a laugh.

Standing That Counts

The man on the corner is ramrodded
and regal as the blue heron
guarding its home in the viburnum.

Who the man is and what he's thinking
is irrelevant—all I want today

is his "I can take anything you dish out"
stance and the accompanying dignity

as I try to ignore the threatening sky
about to piggyback on the light drizzle,

and the bus with its headlights large
as prison beams switched on, rattling
past, down the world of Main Street.

Tim Suermondt

Small Streets

for Yasi

I too love small streets—
those orphans who don't want us
to make a fuss over them
but are delighted when a stranger
shows up and walks through,
by choice or chance. Big History
is never there, though the residents
often display a quiet dignity worthy
of long years note. Birds always
hop on the concrete—the scrawny
trees always seem a little naked
even in a state of bloom, and the moon
always looks like you can capture it,
put it in your pocket and pull it out
whenever you swear it's necessary.

Hopeful in Utrecht Tonight

after Mia Avramut

In this elbow of the world
everything seems to be as it should.

The stubborn daylight that still faintly clings
to the many rooftops attests to this clearly,

and the men and women of the city seem
to have satisfaction woven into their stylish clothes.

I look through the windows of a passing trolley
and can see my friends at work and play in America.

I'm tempted to cross the canal to the park,
pick up a fallen branch and scratch on the sky

"I'll be returning soon" and not worry whether they're
ready or not to welcome me back.

Tim Suermondt

I've Changed Some People Say

And I hope they mean for the better.

I do sense that my eyebrows are on the verge
of blossoming into the dark, black sheen
they haven't had for a long while,

though that nugget, like those far more substantial,
is most likely a manifestation of wishful thinking—

a condition not unknown to me.

Look, good people, I can't save myself,
let alone the world—even David who was blessed
with playing on a ten string instrument failed,

but my wife is beautiful, I still believe that the best
will be victorious over the worst
and I throw perfect football spirals to my neighbor's

son—my deft, cannon arm changing in the autumn light
to the pure, local myth of a legend.

I Stand Almost at the Edge of the Ocean but I Pay It No Attention

I feel slightly ashamed at ignoring
its magnificence, but here I indeed am
staring into the distance where you,
my love, might be at this very moment
sitting on a couch, eating a bowl of noodles,

understanding the power of simplicity
like a prisoner who dreams not of a four
course meal, but of one slice of rye bread
buttered so thin its lack makes one ravenous.
I don't do exile well and waiting for anything

makes me bereft, waiting for you unbearable.
I'll leave when the sun starts to retire, only
to be back in a matter of days to be rude again,
imagining the expanse between us shrinking
as the waves slip further in than out, in solidarity.

Tim Suermondt

Saving the World

I walk in the sunlight,
my wife by my side.

The city is crowd whipped
and we duck into a movie house

on a side street and hide out
like a pair of fugitives

until the coast is clear and dark.
At the harbor we watch the lights

thread the opposite shore, my wife
brushing strands of black hair

from her face just like the actress
we saw too beautiful to forget.

Out of the Dark

Queensland, Australia

This night the ocean is as dark
as Satan's overcoat,

but it all promises to be good—

the full moon, the major light,
surrounded by a bodyguard of clouds

indicates magnificence has arrived.

Tomorrow a dictator will be toppled,
refugees will fit snugly into any country,

pain retreating while recuperation reigns—

and the dudes, on surfboards bright as gold,
will rule, pointing to the perfect

wave even they thought would never come.

Jimmie Collins

He lives in his driveway,
taking apart and putting back
the Chevy's engine,

absolutely absorbed
in the work of oil and grease,
tools and machines

of actual intelligent design
born again every time
he cares for his "green baby"

like he'd care for a real one.
"What do you think of my Cadillac?"
he often asks people walking by,

"Isn't she the best?" Especially
when she's revealed in light,
the red extension cord

plugged in to the moon, wrenched
down by his hard-working, expert
hands so pretty in the execution.

To the Poets Who Won't Get a Drop of Ink When They Die

Cheer up—the poets who will get the ink
won't know it, life's last joke on them.

Be sorry, but celebrate—keep your hands
on the keyboard, pencils pens and paper within

reach as well—the poems, spiteful, beautiful,
demand our attention and don't give a damn

who we are, who we wish we were but will never be.
A magnificent line is somewhere in the room, strutting.

49

Tim Suermondt

The Quiet of Paris

That good French word
langueur rules—

even the schoolchildren
make none

of their customary noise.
At the Pasteur

Institute the work goes on
and I slip

silently into the smallest café
on Montparnasse—

the rain ginning up and birds
readying to land

on my heavy, wobbly table
black as night.

The Tram Turns onto the Last Street

for PK

Going from sunlight into sunlight
on the tracks of generations.

The world is old, the world is new.

A dog bites at the skirt
of a schoolgirl crossing the road,

a girl who will grow up
to be famous and much beloved
(some of us will always be remembered.)

The world is old, the world is new

and there's no time, except time—
even, brightly, on the other side.

Tim Suermondt

It's Only the Universe

new friend greets me
funeral cart passes—
the first star!
　　　　—Andy Jackson

Friends, new and old,
we have a ways to go

before we start considering
that funeral cart..

Let the pizzeria under the night stars
stand for what's vitally important.

Let us keep saving the world
and ourselves while on our barstools.

Let us tramp the cities and islands
so often in our dreams

that we become citizens, inexhaustible.

Inspector Watanabe

In a dream running along a dark,
ramshackle alley in the city
I find the clue that will crack the case.

I wake up, go for my shoes—but my wife,
standing in her bra and panties white
as the morning sun, is slyly dangling
them in front of me.

The murderer has no chance and I prepare
a few maxims for him to contemplate
during his lifelong incarceration:

The liverworts and moss in the parks
hold secrets tighter than their roots

Persistence tied to luck is indomitable

Justice must weigh heavier than the butterfly

I go out into the rain, carrying my umbrella
like a samurai flush with victory
and the stern approval of the gods.

They're Off

The latest book I'm reading flies out of my hands,
out one open window, disappearing down the street ripe

with cars and pedestrians, browning leaves on the trees.
"Books always fly out of your hands," my wife says,

concerned, as if she meant like my life flying away.
"Let's see if we can track it down," I say, "find out where

they've all gone, must be to a place the size of stadiums."
She gets her coat and tosses me my shoes, combs her hair

quickly in front of the parlor mirror. "Can you imagine,"
she says, "the look on their covers when they see you coming?"

The Old Idea of War, 2237

I walk in the park
and watch the dogs,
the children
and the gentle cyborgs,
no dark glove trying
to smother every continent—
history bathes in generosity,
always in the open and beautifully.

Tim Suermondt

It Does Matter

She makes the ordinary
black dress look spectacular,

and those red lips!

What pain am I dealing with?
What tragedy to overcome?

It does matter,
but not tonight.

She takes the dress off,
folds it and lays it

on the books
on the nightstand,

those red lips

mouthing nothing about history
or the lure of philosophy.

Do Some Fishing Along the Seine

But my fishing days are over—
pity for the fish is my excuse.
I stand on a bridge and watch—
all the history and art,
and a group of pretty women
in pretty dresses, all of them cradling
books. I couldn't be happier.

Revolution Street

This afternoon the sun, rather comic like,
is being pricked by antennas on the roofs.
I hear the noise from the vast stadium nearby
and wait for a sizeable portion of the crowd
to invade the street, either in giddy or disconsolate
fashion strictly depending on the outcome.
With wine glass in hand I usually salute everyone,
the winners as well as the losers, the shadows where
boys and girls go to keep cool, the slightest ounce
of plushness I see and invent—even the silly toast
to time and its end hangs supremely in the air.

September

The magnitude of the world is driving me crazy
and I find my respite in a hot dog smeared
with mustard, sauerkraut—beautiful moment of languor
in the City I adore. My first bite—and a mother braiding
her hair in the small house on Court Street, a boy
sitting quietly in the back of a school bus, a big man
playing a saxophone since just after daybreak, the air
charged and charmed around him. I finish the dog
and vanish in the shadows of the shiny, tall buildings.

Piaf

Yes, weather-beaten,
        life-beaten,
        sad.

But in the photo
how strong the trees
look that fall,

the gray Gestapo prison
freshly painted mint,
a school once again.

Edith seems to be saying
"Because it's Paris …"

the moon over Montparnasse
on its way, a flight of stairs
leading to a corner room,

a negligee on the floor,
a song on the radio
that could break your heart

        if you let it.
        Let it.

Marconi Beach

Surrounded by a division of gulls,
shrieking and yapping
like Confederates at Gettysburg—

my feet ecstatic in the muddy sand.

An ocean liner with laborious
elegance riding the water, my
imagination robust, putting me aboard

to walk the decks with a woman
whose auburn hair actually does dance
in the breezy, hot air.

Remembering the boy in school
who was often admonished to avoid
the slightest hint of slothfulness—

"Good thing you never went along"

the woman says, taking off her summer
dress and going to lie on the cabin bed,
looking over my shoulder at the cornucopia

of stars the late night has produced, effortlessly.

Tim Suermondt

Bob Dylan Wins the Nobel Prize

No beef from me,
but I have no guitar and I don't sing.

Maybe literature is a little less stuffy now,
but the fabulous mansion on the hill

will keep calling.

The night has come quickly—
this poem has come quickly too,

but it's still a poem.

Poetry is important wherever it's found.
I haven't forgotten.

Proust

"The Perfect Vandals" ... but of the mind and the heart.
A farm hidden by the sprawling apple orchard,
the Champs-Elysees at the start of the night,
the sound of the bat striking the ball and April
full of catfish under the wayward bridge, the blending
of the concrete and the stars, the planets of the cities beaming.

Tim Suermondt

Shouldn't Be Much to Ask

> *We are not so badly off, if we can*
> *Admire Dutch painting.*
> —Czeslaw Milosz

I want that house of quietude.
I want the fruit and bread on the table.
I want the young woman who takes care
of it all and never loses her beauty.

We'll get married, live for art and each other.
Morning sunlight in winter poking
us in bed as we sleep late, vigorously.
How, how could she ever say no to that?

"Letter to a Young Poet"

Walk around, take the measure of things
no matter how fleeting.
Then sit and start scribing—pen and paper,
computer keyboard, the choice is yours.
Let gratitude introduce itself,
tell loneliness to go to hell, let memories
drop their duffel bags and suitcases anywhere.
Write like the biggest son-of-a-bitch would—
you're writing a poem for Christ's sake.

Tim Suermondt

Spending Part of New Year's Eve Watching a *Three Stooges* Marathon

We all usher in the New Year in our own way,
humbly confident that this will be the best year ever,
last year's litany of disappointments vanished for the moment.

The optimism is justified: Larry eye-poked here, Moe shot out
of a cannon there and everyone still intact and thriving,
pain and mayhem morphing into laughter without any regret.

I haven't done the Curly Shuffle, but I know someone else will,
dancing smartly and stooge-like under a cold white moon,
*nyuk-nyuk*ing for good measure, right before the fireworks.

Waiting for My Wife Who's Gone to Do a Quick Errand

Five seconds. It didn't take long to miss her,
no one does the instants better than me.

It's a cold day and a man down the street
is actually making a bonfire, looking responsible

in the way he starts the flame.
I open the refrigerator, searching for a snack

that is hiding itself well, but I persevere
and find it, untouched, to my delight.

Time quickens with every bite I take, the sound
of a key turning in the door becomes the universe,

my wife arriving fresh as a new planet,
announcing she's back like she never meant to leave.

Tim Suermondt

The Cavalcade of Children

Who can't wait to become grown-ups.
Don't tell them not to hurry—they

won't listen. We never listened.

And speaking of you and me, here
we are in the latter days of Fall,

full-fledged adults, and mature
(well most of the time), preparing

ourselves for a harsh Winter, watching

Children of Paradise while the city
gets quieter with every doomed leaf,

looking again to sleep, yes, like a baby.

After the Election

The sailboats in the darkling marina
remain buttressed for the coming winter,

just feet away from the columns of trees
and the beautiful, dying fall of their leaves.

A man says to a woman "What's changed?"
and she says "How much time ya got?"—

a conversation perfect for the proceedings.
I step on, accidentally I assure you, a poster

of the winning candidate, his name encircled
by white stars, the first humiliation of many

he'll have—though he isn't brilliant enough
to know it as he watches the moon scrape

his penthouse, he thinks, to offer supplication.

Tim Suermondt

The First Day of Summer

The wide spatula of air
whips the clouds into shape
and the trouble following me
has gotten lost. Precisely what
the trouble was I can't say—
let it be mercifully forgotten.

Now I can take a walk around
the entire lake before returning
to the city where I'll greet my wife
and escort her, hand-in-hand,
through the noble and mean streets—
every tough stepping aside gracefully.

Whistle

The dogs (not mine) and I
love to take the path to the train tracks—

love when the Silverliner speeds by,
shocking up our hair while we slowly
close our eyes and dream of realms
as real as they are imagined.

We'd like to abide the entire day,
but we have responsibilities.

The dogs run off, barking.
I neither run nor bark, but trek back down
just as thankful, just as happy.

Tim Suermondt

The World Isn't Ending

Every generation has its flashpoints
which lead to conflagrations, where men,
women and children are strewn about—
and sometimes a dog sitting on the rubble

of a house that could have been anyone's.
But the theologian who wrote "we must
remember the world is also meek and kind"
was right, like driving down the Taconic Parkway

and my wife reminding me of people we knew
who lived in the area, including some friends
I had shamelessly almost forgotten—"Wave
to Lee," she said, executing a brisk wave herself

and adding "The world is beautiful" and it was
for the entire drive—forests and deer, a strange
gift shop selling wooden clogs and the owner's dog
curled in a corner, watching everyone with delight.

Acknowledgments

Poems in this collection have appeared in *MadHat Lit, The Southeast Review, Ploughshares, Mudlark, Galway Review (Ireland), Jam Tarts, Cold Mountain Review, The Peacock Journal, Dewpoint, The Lake Journal* (England), *Blue Heron, Lunch Ticket, Pirene's Fountain, Taos Journal of Poetry and Art, Pinyon Review, Constellations, Mojave River Review, First Literary Review East, Seven Circle Press, Black Bottom Review* (England), *Isthmus Review, Petrichor, One Throne Magazine* (Canada), *OffCourse, Kentucky Review, Ikelftiko* (England), *Autumn Sky Review, Route 7 Review, Hobo Camp Review, Those Fragile Lilacs Journal, Ishann Literary Review, Pure Slush, Hamilton Stone Review, Past Simple, Unlikely Stories,* and *Desde Hong Kong: Poets in Conversation with Octavio Paz,* eds. German Munoz, Tammy Lai-Ming Ho & Juan Jose Morales (Chameleon Press, 2014).

ABOUT THE AUTHOR

TIM SUERMONDT is the author of four full-length collections of poems: *Trying To Help The Elephant Man Dance* (The Backwaters Press, 2007), *Just Beautiful* (New York Quarterly Books, 2010), *Election Night And The Five Satins* (Glass Lyre Press, 2016) and *The World Doesn't Know You* (Pinyon Publishing, 2017). He has poems published in *Poetry, The Georgia Review, Ploughshares, Prairie Schooner, Blackbird, Bellevue Literary Review, North Dakota Quarterly, december magazine, Plume Poetry Journal, Southern Humanities Review* and *Stand Magazine* (England), among others. He lives in Cambridge (MA) with his wife, the poet Pui Ying Wong.